Comparing **Past** and **Present**

Cooking and Eating

Rebecca Rissman

Raintree is an imprint of Capstone Global Library Limited, a company incorporated in England and Wales having its registered office at 7 Pilgrim Street, London, EC4V 6LB – Registered company number: 6695582

www.raintreepublishers.co.uk
myorders@raintreepublishers.co.uk

Text © Capstone Global Library Limited 2014
First published in hardback in 2014
The moral rights of the proprietor have been asserted.

Edited by Rebecca Rissman, Daniel Nunn, and Catherine Veitch
Designed by Philippa Jenkins
Picture research by Elizabeth Alexander
Production by Helen McCreath
Originated by Capstone Global Library Ltd
Printed and bound in China

ISBN 978 1 4062 7146 1
17 16 15 14 13
10 9 8 7 6 5 4 3 2 1

British Library Cataloguing in Publication Data
A full catalogue record for this book is available from the British Library.

Acknowledgements
We would like to thank the following for permission to reproduce photographs: Alamy pp. 4 (© Wolverhampton City Council - Arts and Heritage), 7 (© Blend Images), 12 (© Elizabeth Whiting & Associates); Corbis pp. 8 (A. W. Cutler/National Geographic Society), 20 (© Minnesota Historical Society); Getty Images pp. 10 (Hulton Archive), 14 (Chicago History Museum), 16 (Haywood Magee/Picture Post/Hulton Archive), 18 (Gerry Cranham/Fox Photos), 23 (Hulton Archive); Shutterstock pp. 5 (© wavebreakmedia), 9 (© Gr8), 11 (© Tatjana Kruusma), 13 (© Yeko Photo Studio), 15 (© kazoka), 19 (© Monkey Business Images), 21 (© Kzenon), 23 (© Tatjana Kruusma), 23 (© kazoka); Superstock pp. 6, 17 (age footstock), 22.

Front cover photographs of two girls making doughnuts, 1925, reproduced with permission of Corbis (© Bettmann), and a woman using an electric mixer reproduced with permission of Getty Images (Nacivet/Photographer's Choice). Back cover photograph of a woman and children cooking reproduced with permission of Superstock.

We would like to thank Nancy Harris and Diana Bentley for their invaluable help in the preparation of this book.

Contents

Comparing the past and present

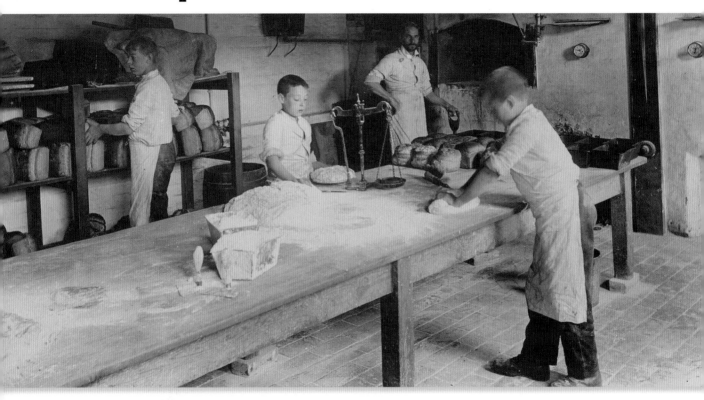

Things in the past have already happened.

Things in the present are happening now.

Cooking has changed over time.

The way people cook today
is very different to the past.

Kitchens

In the past some kitchens were outdoors.

Today, most kitchens are indoors.

Kitchen appliances

In the past ovens were heated by burning wood.

Today, some ovens are heated
by electricity.

In the past people did not
have fridges. They kept food for
a short time.

Today, people have fridges. They can keep food for a longer time.

In the past some people did not have running water. They pumped water from under the ground.

Today, people get running water
from the tap.

Cooking

In the past cooking meals took a long time.

Today, people can cook a meal
in a short time.

Getting food

In the past some people grew vegetables to eat. Some people also kept animals to eat.

Today, people buy most of their food from shops.

Eating food

In the past people ate food that was grown where they lived.

Today, people eat food from around the world.

Then and now

In the past many children helped cook meals. Today, many children still help cook meals.

Picture glossary

 electricity power that makes machines work

 oven kitchen tool used to cook food

 running water water that flows from a tap

Index

Notes for parents and teachers

Before reading

Talk to children about the difference between the past and present. Explain that the conversation you are having with them is taking place in the present. Then ask children to remember what they did last week. Explain that those activities took place in the past.

After reading

- Explain to children that the way people cook has changed over time. Ask children to name one or two of their favourite foods. Then, as a group, brainstorm about how the preparation method may have changed over time (e.g. in the past, people would not have purchased cake mix from the shop; in the past, people might have kept their own chickens for eggs, etc.).

- Ask children to make a list of common kitchen equipment, such as microwaves, fridges, and mixers. Once children have finished their lists, ask them to cross off every item that would not have existed 100 years ago. Discuss their answers with the group.

- Ask children to turn to pages 16–17. Ask them to make a list of differences between the images. Record their observations on the board. As a group, discuss how cooking has changed over time.